Kim Helps Out

written by Jay Dale

illustrated by Cherie Zamazing

"Kim!" shouted Dad
from the back door.
"Can you please come inside
and help?
Tom is making a **big** mess."

2

Kim was outside in the garden.
She was looking at a book.

"Yes, Dad," said Kim.
"I can come inside and help."

Kim got up and walked inside.

"Oh, Tom!" she cried.

"You **have** made a big mess!"

7

Kim saw lots of paper on the floor.
She saw lots of pencils, too.

"I'm making a birthday card
for Mum," said Tom.
"She will be home at two o'clock."

9

Kim looked at the big mess.

Then she looked at the clock.

"Come on," she said.

"Let's get going!

We have a birthday card

to make."

11

Kim helped Dad and Tom
to make the birthday card.
It was a big blue card.

"Look!" said Kim.
"I can see lots of stickers
in this red tin.
They can go on the card."

They all made Mum
a pop-up card.
It had ten yellow flowers inside.
It had lots of stickers, too.

"Happy Birthday!" shouted Dad.

"Happy Birthday, Mum!"

shouted Kim and Tom.